CHILDREN'S
PARTY·CAKES

Corinne Mitchell

J. B. FAIRFAX

CONTENTS

Project editor Katie Swallow
Edited by Barbara Croxford
Designed by Maggie Aldred
Photography by James Duncan

Typeset by J&L Composition Ltd, Filey, North Yorkshire
Colour separation by Fotographics Ltd, UK–Hong Kong
Printed in Italy by New Interlitho S.p.A.

Published in 1992 by Merehurst Ltd, Ferry House, 51–57 Lacy Road,
Putney, London SW15 1PR

Distributed by J.B. Fairfax Press Ltd, 9 Trinity Centre, Park Farm,
Wellingborough, Northants NN8 6ZB

Copyright © Merehurst Ltd 1992

ISBN 1–874567–20–4

NOTES ON USING THE RECIPES
Quantities are given in metric, Imperial and cups. Follow one set of
measures only as they are not interchangeable.
American terms have been included as necessary throughout, given in
brackets following the UK name.

INTRODUCTION

Children's Party Cakes introduces 'Inlaid Icing', a new and exciting technique for creating novelty cakes with a difference. With this technique the design is transferred onto a sugarpasted cake by pricking through tracings made from the templates provided. Each piece of the design is then cut from the cake top and replaced by coloured sugarpaste.

Using this simple technique and easy to use sugarpaste you just can't go wrong, and there's no need to buy expensive equipment – a modelling knife, plastic smoother, pearl/glass head pins and greaseproof (parchment) paper are all you need to get started.

Children's Party Cakes contains easy to make cake recipes, including a light fresh Orange and Lemon Madeira, a rich moist Chocolate Chip and Walnut Cake and a colourful and mouthwatering Cherry and Coconut Cake.

These outstanding designs have been created to give the maximum effect with minimum work, each with clear step by step instructions and colour photographs.

CORINNE MITCHELL

For further designs using this effective technique, look out for the book Easy Party Cakes. *Containing over 20 cakes for all occasions, it is available from good bookshops. For further information on stockists, write to the address shown on the back of this book.*

CAKE RECIPES

CHOCOLATE CHIP AND WALNUT CAKE

Tin (pan) size	15cm (6in) square 18cm (7in) round	18cm (7in) square 20cm (8in) round	20cm (8in) square 23cm (9in) round	23cm (9in) square 25cm (10in) round
Butter	125g (4oz/½ cup)	155g (5oz/⅔ cup)	220g (7oz/⅞ cup)	280g (9oz/scant 1¼ cups)
Soft light brown sugar	90g (3oz/½ cup)	125g (4oz/⅔ cup)	185g (6oz/1 cup)	250g (8oz/1⅓ cups)
Golden (corn) syrup	30ml (2tbsp)	30ml (2tbsp)	45ml (3tbsp)	45ml (3tbsp)
Eggs	2	2	4	5
Self-raising flour	220g (7oz/1¾ cups)	280g (9oz/2¼ cups)	375g (12oz/3 cups)	500g (1lb/4 cups)
Milk	45ml (3tbsp)	60–75ml (4–5tbsp)	75–90ml (5–6tbsp)	75–90ml (5–6tbsp)
Plain (semisweet) chocolate chips or plain cooking chocolate cut into pieces	90g (3oz/¾ cup)	90g (3oz/¾ cup)	125g (4oz/1 cup)	155g (5oz/1¼ cups)
Walnuts, chopped	90g (3oz/¾ cup)	90g (3oz/¾ cup)	125g (4oz/1 cup)	155g (5oz/1¼ cups)
Baking time	50–55mins	1hr 5mins	1hr 10mins	1hr 15mins

1. Preheat the oven to 180°C/350°F/Gas 4.
2. Grease and line the correct size tin (pan).
3. Cream the butter and sugar together in a bowl until light and fluffy.
4. Beat in the syrup.
5. Beat in the eggs, one at a time.
6. Sift the flour and add to the egg mixture, mixing until smooth and creamy.
7. Stir in the milk.

8. Add the chocolate chips and walnuts, stirring until evenly mixed.
9. Turn the mixture into the prepared tin (pan). Bake for the appropriate time or until well risen and a fine skewer inserted into the centre comes out clean.
10. Leave in the tin for 10 minutes, then turn out onto a wire rack to cool.

VARIATIONS

For an all chocolate chip cake, simply omit the walnuts.

Instead of using walnuts, substitute the same amount of chopped hazelnuts.

NOTE
For a fan assisted oven, check the cake 10 minutes before the end of the stated baking time. This applies to all the cakes.

CHERRY AND COCONUT CAKE

Tin (pan) size	15cm (6in) square 18cm (7in) round	18cm (7in) square 20cm (8in) round	20cm (8in) square 23cm (9in) round	23cm (9in) square 25cm (10in) round
Glacé (candied) cherries, quartered	185g (6oz/1 cup)	250g (8oz/1⅓ cups)	250g (8oz/1⅓ cups)	315g (10oz/1⅔ cups)
Desiccated (shredded) coconut	60g (2oz/⅔ cup)	60g (2oz/⅔ cup)	90g (3oz/1 cup)	125g (4oz/1⅓ cups)
Self-raising flour	315g (10oz/2½ cups)	375g (12oz/3 cups)	500g (1lb/4 cups)	625g (1¼lb/5 cups)
Salt	pinch	pinch	1.25ml (¼ tsp)	1.25ml (¼ tsp)
Butter	125g (4oz/½ cup)	185g (6oz/¾ cup)	315g (10oz/1¼ cups)	375g (12oz/1½ cups)
Caster (superfine) sugar	125g (4oz/½ cup)	185g (6oz/¾ cup)	315g (10oz/1¼ cups)	375g (12oz/1½ cups)
Eggs	3	4	5	6
Milk	60–75ml (4–5 tbsp)	75–90ml (5–6 tbsp)	90–105ml (6–7 tbsp)	105–120ml (7–8tbsp)
Baking time	1hr 15mins	1hr 15–20mins	1hr 20–30mins	1hr 25–35mins

1. Preheat the oven to 180°C/350°F/Gas 4.
2. Grease and line the correct size tin (pan).
3. Wash and dry the cherries, then mix with the coconut.
4. Sift the flour and salt into a bowl.
5. Cut the butter into small cubes and rub into the flour until it resembles fine breadcrumbs.
6. Add the sugar, coconut and cherries, stirring lightly to mix.
7. Beat the eggs and milk together, then stir into the mixture.
8. Turn the mixture into the prepared tin (pan). Bake for the appropriate time or until well risen and a fine skewer inserted into the centre comes out clean.
9. Leave in the tin for 10 minutes, then turn out onto a wire rack to cool.

ORANGE AND LEMON MADEIRA

Tin (pan) size	15cm (6in) square 18cm (7in) round	18cm (7in) square 20cm (8in) round	20cm (8in) square 23cm (9in) round	23cm (9in) square 25cm (10in) round
Self-raising flour	185g (6oz/1½ cups)	250g (8oz/2 cups)	315g (10oz/2½ cups)	375g (12oz/3 cups)
Plain (all-purpose) flour	90g (3oz/¾ cup)	125g (4oz/1 cup)	155g (5oz/1¼ cups)	185g (6oz/1½ cups)
Butter	185g (6oz/¾ cup)	250g (8oz/1 cup)	315g (10oz/1¼ cups)	375g (12oz/1½ cups)
Caster (superfine) sugar	185g (6oz/¾ cup)	250g (8oz/1 cup)	315g (10oz/1¼ cups)	375g (12oz/1½ cups)
Eggs	3	4	5	6
Grated orange rind and juice	½	½	½–1	1
Grated lemon rind and juice	½	½	½–1	1
Baking time	1 hr 15 mins	1hr 20mins	1hr 25–30mins	1hr 25–30mins

1. Preheat the oven to 160°C/325°F/Gas 3.
2. Grease and line the correct size tin (pan).
3. Sift the flours together.
4. Cream the butter and sugar together in a bowl until very pale and fluffy.
5. Add one egg plus a spoonful of flour at a time, beating well between each addition.
6. Fold in the remaining flour.
7. Stir in enough orange and lemon juice to give a firm but dropping consistency.
8. Stir in the orange and lemon rind.
9. Turn the mixture into the prepared tin (pan). Bake for the appropriate time or until well risen.
10. Leave in the tin for 10 minutes, then turn out onto a wire rack to cool.

COVERING THE CAKE

Covering a Cake with Marzipan

To successfully cover a cake with sugarpaste the edges and corners should be smooth and well rounded, this is achieved by applying the marzipan in one piece. By kneading liquid glycerine (glycerol) into the marzipan it becomes more pliable and easier to work with, which is necessary when applying marzipan this way.

1 Brush a small amount of apricot jam on the centre of the cake board to secure the cake.

2 Level the top of the cake and place upside down on the cake board. If the base edges are not level with the board, make a roll of marzipan to fit the gap, and press into place using a palette knife or a plastic smoother. Fill in any dents and repair any broken corners and edges with marzipan, securing with apricot glaze if necessary.

3 Brush over the cake with apricot glaze.

4 On a surface lightly dusted with icing (confectioner's) sugar, knead the liquid glycerine into the marzipan until smooth and pliable, keeping creases on the underside.

5 Roll out to a thickness of 5mm ($\frac{1}{4}$in) and large enough to cover the whole cake.

6 Using a rolling pin or your hands for support, drape the marzipan over the cake and fan out at the base. Using downward strokes, ease the marzipan to fit the sides without creasing.

7 Trim away the excess at the base with a sharp knife, then use a plastic smoother to remove any dents made whilst working.

Square cake: When covering a square cake, prepare as before. Drape the marzipan over the cake and fan out at the base, cupping your hands to fit the corners carefully ease the marzipan into place. Using downward strokes, press the marzipan against the sides without creasing, then trim away excess at the base with a sharp knife. Use a plastic smoother to remove any dents.

The same 'cupped hand' technique is used when covering a square cake with sugarpaste.

Apricot Glaze

45ml (3tbsp) apricot jam
10ml (2tsp) boiled water

1 Place the apricot jam in a saucepan and heat gently until melted, or heat in a microwave for about 1 minute on High.

2 Remove from the heat and stir in the water. Strain through a sieve to remove the fruit. Allow the glaze to cool before use.

MARZIPAN QUANTITY CHART

Cake size	15cm (6in) square 18cm (7in) round	18cm (7in) square 20cm (8in) round	20cm (8in) square 23cm (9in) round	23cm (9in) square 25cm (10in) round
Marzipan	375g (12oz)	500g (1lb)	750g (1½lb)	1kg (2lb)
Liquid glycerine (glycerol)	5ml (1tsp)	5ml (1tsp)	7.5ml (1½ tsp)	10 ml (2tsp)

Covering a Cake with Sugarpaste

When covering a cake with sugarpaste for 'inlaid' decoration, use cooled boiled water to dampen the marzipan on the *sides* of the cake only. This ensures the area on top to be inlaid is kept dry and the cut out sections can be removed easily.

Sugarpaste

Makes 500g (1lb) sugarpaste
45ml (3tbsp) liquid glucose
22.5ml (1½tbsp) powdered gelatine
(unflavored gelatin)
60ml (4tbsp) boiling water
15ml (1tbsp) liquid glycerine (glycerol)
500g (1lb/3½ cups) icing (confectioner's)
sugar
cornflour (cornstarch) for dusting

1 Stand the jar of liquid glucose in a bowl of boiling water for 5–10 minutes to soften. Half-fill a saucepan with water, heat to boiling point, then remove from the heat. Place the gelatine and boiling water in a heatproof bowl over the saucepan of hot water, stir constantly until the gelatine dissolves. Add the liquid glucose and glycerine, then stir until completely blended. Allow to cool for 5 minutes.
2 Sift the icing (confectioner's) sugar into a large mixing bowl and make a well in the centre.
3 Pour the gelatine mixture into the well. Stir with a wooden spoon, gradually drawing in the icing sugar from the side of the bowl, until the mixture becomes stiff and forms a ball.
4 Place the sugarpaste on a surface dusted with cornflour (cornstarch) and knead until smooth, pliable and no longer sticky, dusting the surface with more cornflour if necessary. Store in a polythene bag or cling film (plastic wrap) until needed.

1

On a surface dusted with icing (confectioner's) sugar, knead the sugarpaste until smooth and pliable, keeping the creases on the underside. Roll out the sugarpaste to a thickness of 2.5 mm (⅛in) and large enough to cover the whole cake. Using your hands for support, drape the sugarpaste over the cake.

Although sugarpaste can be made at home, the bought varieties available in most supermarkets are excellent and of a very high standard.

2

Fan out the sugarpaste at the base away from the sides of the cake then, with the palms of your hands and using downward strokes, ease the sugarpaste to fit the sides without creasing.

3

Trim away excess sugarpaste at the base with a sharp knife, then use a plastic smoother to remove any dents. With your hands free from icing (confectioner's) sugar, gently rub over the cake top with circular movements for a smooth and glossy finish.

Colours and Colouring Sugarpaste

Paste colours are ideal for colouring sugarpaste, as it is possible to create both subtle and darker shades without changing the consistency of the sugarpaste. Specialist cake decorating shops carry a wide range of these paste food colours.

Colouring Sugarpaste

Sugarpaste is best coloured in natural light as artificial light can affect colour perception. When this light is not possible, daylight simulation light bulbs can help, these are available from most art and craft shops.

Using a cocktail stick (toothpick), add a small amount of paste colour to the sugarpaste and knead until the colour is even and no longer streaky. Add more colour if needed or more sugarpaste if the colour is too dark. Seal in a polythene bag or cling film (plastic wrap).

Marbling: For a marbled effect, gently knead the colour into the sugarpaste and leave streaky. For subtle marbling only use a small amount of colour or a larger amount for a more dramatic effect (see also page 20).

Mixing Colours

Although there are many colours of paste food colouring available, it is possible to blend two colours together to create another. For this you will need five basic colours only – green (blue in tone), red, yellow, blue (turquoise in tone) and pink. These basic colours can be used in smaller or larger amounts to create both paler and darker shades of the basic colour (see Colour Chart on page 10).

The secondary colours shown on the colour chart are created by blending the colours above and below the basic colours in equal proportions, for example: to mix 125g (4oz) of colour No. 19 pale basic blue + pale basic pink, colour 60g (2oz) sugarpaste pale blue and 60g (2oz) pale pink, then knead the two colours together until completely blended.

Liquid Food Colours

Liquid food colourings can also be used to colour sugarpaste. The liquid food colours available in most major supermarkets are not as rich in colour as those sold in specialist cake decorating shops. It will not be possible to create the darker colours shown on the colour chart with these liquid colours, but pale basic and basic colours can be mixed as above.

If the liquid food colouring you are using does not have a dropper, tip a small amount of the liquid into a bowl and use a teaspoon to add the liquid to the sugarpaste in small amounts. To prevent the sugarpaste from becoming wet and sticky, add the liquid colour one or two drops at a time and knead thoroughly. Should the sugarpaste become sticky, knead in icing (confectioner's) sugar until it returns to a normal consistency.

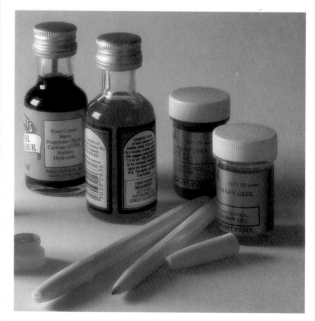

1 pale basic green
2 basic green
3 dark basic green
4 pale basic red
5 basic red
6 basic red + dark basic green
7 pale basic red + pale basic yellow
8 basic red + basic yellow + white sugarpaste
9 basic red + dark yellow
10 pale basic yellow
11 basic yellow
12 dark basic yellow
13 pale basic yellow + pale basic blue
14 basic yellow + basic blue
15 dark basic yellow + dark basic blue
16 pale basic blue
17 basic blue
18 dark basic blue
19 pale basic blue + pale basic pink
20 basic blue + basic pink
21 dark basic blue + dark basic pink
22 pale basic pink
23 basic pink
24 dark basic pink

INLAID ICING TECHNIQUE

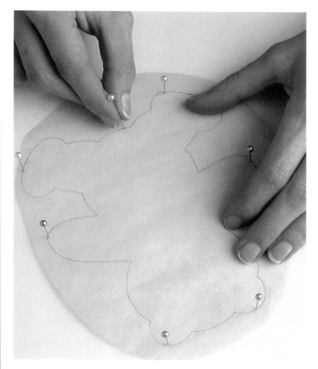

1

Trace the design templates onto sheets of greaseproof (parchment) paper, then trim the paper to fit the cake top. Keeping the areas to be inlaid dry, roll out the sugarpaste to 2.5mm ($\frac{1}{8}$in) and cover the cake.

Position tracing A on the cake top and secure with pearl or glass headed pins on the *inside* edge of the pencil line. Using a pin, mark through the tracing every 2.5mm ($\frac{1}{8}$in) on the *inside* edge of the pencil line, then remove the tracing.

2

Using a modelling knife, cut the section from the sugarpaste, cutting on the *outside* edge of the pin marks. Carefully lift the section from the cake top.

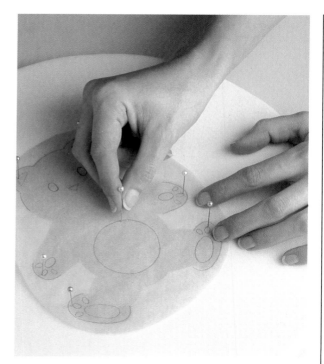

3

Roll out the appropriate coloured sugarpaste to 2.5mm (⅛in) on a surface dusted with icing (confectioner's) sugar. Holding the same tracing (A) in position, transfer the design by using a pin to mark through the tracing every 2.5mm (⅛in) on the *outside* edge of the pencil line, then remove the tracing.

There will be two lines of marks, the holes that have just been made and dents from the previous transfer. Cut the section out, cutting between the two lines of marks. Lift out the section and inlay into the cake top, using your fingers to smooth over the coloured sugarpaste until the two cut edges meet and the small dents disappear.

4

Using the coloured registration line to ensure the correct position (see page 26), place tracing B on the cake top and secure with pearl or glass headed pins on the *inside* edge of the pencil line. Using a pin, mark through the tracing every 2.5mm (⅛in) on the *inside* edge of the pencil line, then remove the tracing.

> To check if your coloured sugarpaste is the same thickness as the sugarpaste on the cake, cut a small strip from the edge of the rolled out coloured paste. Take the section that has just been cut from the cake top and lay it along the cut edge. If the coloured sugarpaste is too thin, knead into a ball and roll out again. If it is too thick roll out until the two cut edges match.

5

Roll out the appropriate coloured sugarpaste to 2.5mm ($\frac{1}{8}$in) on a surface dusted with icing (confectioner's) sugar. Hold tracing B in position, using a pin, mark through the tracing every 2.5mm ($\frac{1}{8}$in) on the *outside* edge of the pencil line. Cut each section of the design from the cake top and inlay with the appropriate coloured section, using your fingers to smooth over the coloured sugarpaste until the two cut edges meet and the small dents disappear. Only cut out and inlay one section at a time.

When all the sections have been completed, gently smooth over the cake top with a plastic smoother to remove any dents made whilst working.

6

Repeat the procedure for tracings C and D as the design requires, using the coloured registration line to ensure the correct position. When all the sections have been completed, lightly dust the cake top with icing (confectioner's) sugar and use a plastic smoother to remove any dents.

If the sugarpaste appears dry or cracked from the icing sugar, cover with cling film (plastic wrap) for 2–3 hours until the icing sugar has been absorbed.

CUDDLES

This charming teddy bear cake for a young child is also featured on pages 11–13. If necessary, the number on the bear's tummy can be altered to the appropriate age (see page 32).

18cm (7in) or 20cm (8in) round or square cake of your choice, see pages 4–5

•

marzipan to cover cake

•

750g (1½lb) sugarpaste

•

yellow, brown and red paste food colours

•

icing (confectioner's) sugar to dust

•

brown edible food colour pen

•

ribbon and candles to decorate, optional

1 Cover the cake with marzipan, see page 6, then allow to dry in a warm place for 24 hours. Trace the templates from page 26 onto grease-proof (parchment) paper, then trim the paper to fit the cake top.
2 Colour 185g (6oz) sugarpaste yellow, 15g (½oz) brown and 30g (1oz) red, keep aside 15g (½oz) white. Roll out the remaining sugarpaste to 2.5mm (⅛in) and cover the cake, see pages 7–8.
3 Secure tracing A (teddy) in position on the cake top, transfer the design then remove the tracing. Cut out the teddy and inlay with yellow sugarpaste.
4 Secure tracing B (tummy, face and paws) in position, transfer the design then remove the tracing. Cut out the tummy and inlay with white sugarpaste. Cut out the facial features and inlay with brown sugarpaste. Cut out the paws and inlay with brown sugarpaste.
5 Secure tracing C (number and bow) in position, transfer the design then remove the tracing. Cut out the number and inlay with red sugarpaste. Cut out the bow and inlay with red sugarpaste.
6 Lightly dust the cake top with icing (confectioner's) sugar and use a smoother to remove any dents. Allow the sugarpaste to dry for 24–48 hours or until completely dry and will not dent when pressed.
7 Trace teddy's mouth onto greaseproof paper, then using a coloured crayon trace the outline of teddy's nose and eyes to use as a registration line. Hold the tracing in position on the cake top, pressing gently, carefully re-trace over the pencil lines then remove the tracing. Use the brown edible food colour pen to draw in teddy's mouth from the impression left. Decorate with ribbon and candles if using.

Inlaying teddy (tracing A) in yellow sugarpaste.

HETTY, BETTY AND BABY BOO

A pretty cake for a little birthday boy or girl. As with all the cakes, this design can be personalized by adding an appropriate number of candles and coloured ribbon.

20cm (8in) or 23cm (9in) square cake of your choice, see pages 4–5

•

marzipan to cover cake

•

750g (1½lb) sugarpaste

•

black, pink and blue paste food colours

•

icing (confectioner's) sugar to dust

•

ribbon and candles to decorate, optional

1 Cover the cake with marzipan, see page 6, then allow to dry in a warm place for 24 hours. Trace the templates from page 27 onto grease-proof (parchment) paper, then trim the paper to fit the cake top.

2 Colour 125g (4oz) sugarpaste grey, 60g (2oz) pink and 60g (2oz) blue. Roll out the remaining sugarpaste to 2.5mm (⅛in) and cover the cake, see pages 7–8.

3 Secure tracing A (elephants and balloons) in position on the cake top, transfer the design then remove the tracing. Cut out the elephants and inlay with grey sugarpaste. Cut out the balloons and inlay one with pink sugarpaste and the other with blue sugarpaste.

4 Secure tracing B (blankets) in position, transfer the design then remove the tracing. Cut out the large blankets and inlay with pink sugarpaste. Cut out the small blanket and inlay with blue sugarpaste.

5 Hold tracing C (spots and balloon strings) in position, transfer the design then remove the tracing. Cut out the spots on the pink blankets and inlay with blue sugarpaste. Cut out the spot on the blue blanket and inlay with pink sugarpaste. Cut out the balloon strings and inlay with pink and blue sugarpaste.

6 Using a cocktail stick (toothpick) make small dents for the elephants' eyes and fill with small balls of blue sugarpaste.

7 Lightly dust the cake top with icing (confectioner's) sugar and use a smoother to remove any dents. Decorate with ribbon and candles.

To save time when filling small circular sections, make small balls of appropriate coloured sugarpaste, then gently press into place and smooth over.

BRULEE

This friendly dog will delight children
of all ages. Vary the colour of the
dog if liked so the cake relates to a
special pet.

*20cm (8in) or 23cm (9in) square cake of
your choice, see pages 4–5*

•

marzipan to cover cake

•

875g (1¾lb) sugarpaste

•

blue, black and red paste food colours

•

icing (confectioner's) sugar to dust

•

ribbon and candles to decorate, optional

1 Cover the cake with marzipan, see page 6, then allow to dry in a warm place for 24 hours. Trace the templates from page 28 onto greaseproof (parchment) paper, then trim the paper to fit the cake top.

2 Colour 220g (7oz) sugarpaste blue, 125g (4oz) black, 7g (¼oz) red and set aside 100g (3½oz) white. Roll out the remaining sugarpaste to 2.5mm (⅛in) and cover the cake, see pages 7–8.

3 Secure the inset tracing in position on the cake top, transfer the inset outline then remove the tracing. Cut out the inset and inlay with blue sugarpaste.

4 Secure tracing A (body and ears) in position, transfer the design then remove the tracing. Cut out the body and inlay with black sugarpaste. Cut out the ears and inlay with white sugarpaste.

5 Secure tracing B (bib, face and tongue) in position, transfer the design then remove the tracing. Cut out the bib and inlay with white sugarpaste. Cut out the face and inlay with white sugarpaste. Cut out the tongue and inlay with red sugarpaste.

6 Hold tracing C (eyes and nose) in position, transfer the design then remove the tracing. Cut out the eyes and inlay with blue sugarpaste. Cut out the nose and inlay with black sugarpaste.

7 Hold tracing D (eye centres) in position, transfer the design then remove the tracing. Cut out the eye centres and inlay with black sugarpaste.

8 Lightly dust the cake top with icing (confectioner's) sugar and use a smoother to remove any dents. Decorate with ribbon and candles if using.

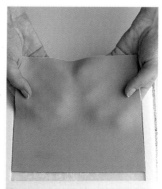

Starting at the top edge, lay the coloured inset into place, then using your hands smooth outwards from the centre until all the cut edges meet. Use a plastic smoother to remove any dents.

DINO

A jolly dinosaur and a seven-year-old make
the perfect partners. Of course, you can
substitute any number for the age required
(see page 32).

*20cm (8in) or 23cm (9in) square cake of
your choice, see pages 4–5*

•

marzipan to cover cake

•

1kg (2lb) sugarpaste

•

yellow, green and orange paste food colours

•

icing (confectioner's) sugar to dust

•

ribbon and candles to decorate, optional

1 Cover the cake with marzipan, see page 6,
then allow to dry in a warm place for 24 hours.
Trace the templates from page 29 onto grease-
proof (parchment) paper, then trim the paper
to fit the cake top.
2 Colour 185g (6oz) sugarpaste yellow then
marble with green paste food colour, colour
185g (6oz) orange. Roll out the remaining
sugarpaste to 2.5mm ($\frac{1}{8}$in) and cover the cake,
see pages 7–8.
3 Secure tracing A (number 7) in position on
the cake top, transfer the design then remove
the tracing. Cut out the number 7 and inlay
with orange sugarpaste.
4 Secure tracing B (Dino) in position, transfer
the design then remove the tracing. Cut out
Dino and inlay with marbled sugarpaste.
5 Hold tracing C (teeth and eye) in position,
transfer the design then remove the tracing.
Cut out the teeth and inlay with white sugarpaste. Cut out the eye and inlay with orange

sugarpaste. Using a pin head, make a dent in
eye centre and fill with a ball of marbled
sugarpaste.
6 Lightly dust the cake top with icing (confectioner's) sugar and use a smoother to remove
any dents. Decorate with ribbon and candles if
using.

Colour the sugarpaste
yellow then add green
paste food colour on a
cocktail stick
(toothpick). Fold the
sugarpaste up and roll
between the hands,
twisting and turning to
create a marbled effect,
adding more colour if
necessary.

TURBO CHARGER

A stunning design for a motorbike fanatic.
The colours can be altered to match a
particular bike (see the colour chart on
page 10).

*23cm (9in) square cake of your choice, see
pages 4–5*

•

marzipan to cover cake

•

1kg (2lb) sugarpaste

•

*red, yellow, black and blue paste food
colours*

•

icing (confectioner's) sugar to dust

•

ribbon and candles to decorate, optional

1 Cover the cake with marzipan, see page 6, then allow to dry in a warm place for 24 hours. Trace the templates from page 30 onto grease-proof (parchment) paper, then trim the paper to fit the cake top.

2 Colour 125g (4oz) sugarpaste red, 60g (2oz) yellow, 60g (2oz) grey, 30g (1oz) light blue and 30g (1oz) dark blue. Roll out the remaining sugarpaste to 2.5mm ($\frac{1}{8}$in) and cover the cake, see pages 7–8.

3 Secure tracing A (bike and wheels) in position on the cake top, transfer the design then remove the tracing. Cut out the bike sections and inlay with red sugarpaste. Cut out the small bike sections and inlay with yellow sugarpaste. Cut out the wheels and inlay with grey sugarpaste.

4 Secure tracing B (rider, centre wheels, petrol tank, bike detail) in position, transfer the design then remove the tracing. Cut out the boot and inlay with grey sugarpaste. Cut out the leg and inlay with light blue sugarpaste. Cut out the body and inlay with dark blue sugarpaste. Cut out the helmet and inlay with red sugarpaste. Cut out the visor and inlay with grey sugarpaste. Cut out the petrol tank and inlay with yellow sugarpaste. Cut out the centre wheels and inlay with yellow sugarpaste. Cut out the bike detail and inlay with white sugarpaste.

5 Hold tracing C (flash on helmet) in position, transfer the design then remove the tracing. Cut out the flash and inlay with pale blue sugarpaste.

6 Lightly dust the cake top with icing (confectioner's) sugar and use a smoother to remove any dents. Decorate with ribbon and candles if using.

When all the sections have been completed, lightly dust cake top with icing (confectioner's) sugar and use a plastic smoother to remove any dents.

TROJAN CLOUD

Making a very effective use of marbled
sugarpaste, here is a celebration cake perfect
for a horse-lover. This dramatic design is
one of the easiest to do!

23cm (9in) square cake of your choice, see
pages 4–5

•

marzipan to cover cake

•

750g (1½lb) sugarpaste

•

black paste food colour

•

icing (confectioner's) sugar to dust

•

ribbon and candles to decorate, optional

1 Cover the cake with marzipan, see page 6,
then allow to dry in a warm place for 24 hours.
Trace the templates from page 31 onto grease-
proof (parchment) paper, then trim the paper
to fit the cake top.

2 Marble 220g (7oz) sugarpaste grey using
black paste food colour (see pages 9 and 20)
and colour 30g (1oz) sugarpaste black. Roll
out the remaining sugarpaste to 2.5mm (⅛in)
and cover the cake, see pages 7–8.

3 Secure tracing A (horse and horse-shoe) in
position on the cake top, transfer the design
then remove the tracing. Cut out the horse-
shoe and inlay with marbled sugarpaste. Cut
out the horse and inlay with marbled sugarpaste. Cut out the mane and inlay with black
sugarpaste. Cut out the tail and inlay with
black sugarpaste.

4 Secure tracing B (horse-shoe nails) in position, transfer design then remove tracing. Cut
out nails and inlay with black sugarpaste.

5 Lightly dust the cake top with icing (confectioner's) sugar and use a smoother to remove
any dents. Decorate with ribbon and candles if
using.

Supporting the horse-
shoe with your hands,
lay it in position on
the cake top easing the
top edges and corners
into place first, then lay
the curved section
into place. Smooth
over until the cut
edges meet.

TEMPLATES

Each template is shown by a different coloured line. Make a separate tracing of each template (A, B, C, D) onto greaseproof (parchment) paper using a pencil, then trim off the excess paper to fit the cake top.

When tracing templates B, C and D, it will help to draw registration lines in a different-coloured pen or crayon by tracing sections from the top and bottom of either template A or the previous template. Then, when placing these tracings on the cake top, simply make sure the coloured registration lines are in the correct position over the coloured inlaid sections.

CUDDLES
page 14

Template A	· · · · · · · · · · · ·
Template B	- - - - - - - - -
Template C	————————
Template D	————————
Features to draw	————————

HETTY, BETTY
AND BABY BOO
page 16

BRULEE
page 18

Template A	····························
Template B	─ ─ ─ ─ ─ ─ ─ ─
Template C	────────────
Template D	────────────
Features to draw	────────────

CAKE TOP INSET

DINO
page 20

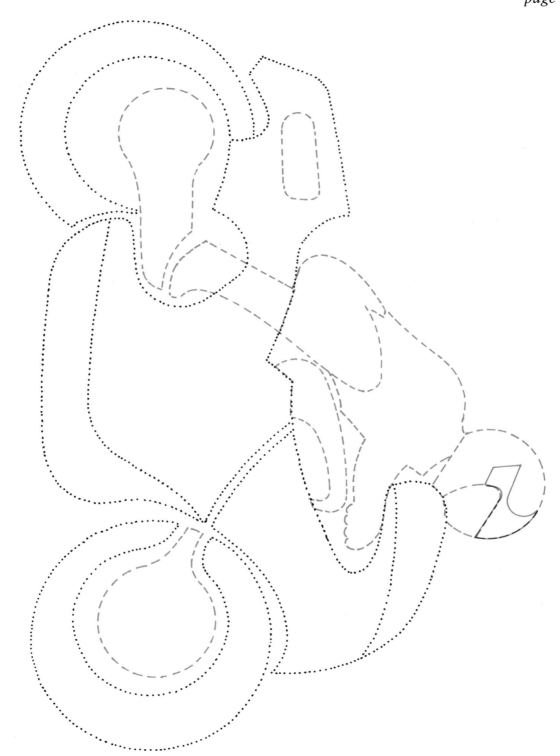

Template A	··················
Template B	– – – – – – – –
Template C	——————
Template D	——————
Features to draw	——————

TROJAN CLOUD
page 24

NUMBERS

Use these numbers as templates when substituting or adding to the cake design. If a larger or smaller number is required, trace off the number shown here onto a sheet of tracing paper or copy paper, using a black felt tip pen to draw the outline. Enlarge or reduce on a suitable photocopier.

1 2 3 4 5

6 7 8 9 0

1 2 3 4 5

6 7 8 9 0